To Elizabeth, Love

GW00786554

This book belongs to:

_____

First paperback edition March 2022

Written and Illustrated by Jessica Roalf

ISBN: 978-1-3999-2473-3

www.jessicaroalf.com

# Luna goes to SPACE!

Written and Illustrated by Jessica Roalf

This is Luna.

She loves Space.

"I wonder what it would be like to actually GO there," she wonders.

She **suddenly** spots her old

'**bouncing boots**' she got for Christmas.

She **then** has an idea...

She will BOUNCE into SPACE!

But first,

she

needs

a

Spacesuit.

...so she **makes** one.

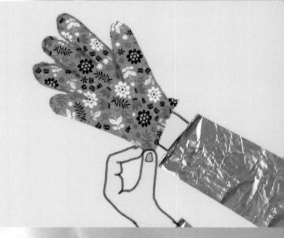

Then, she goes into her garden, bends her knees...

AND...

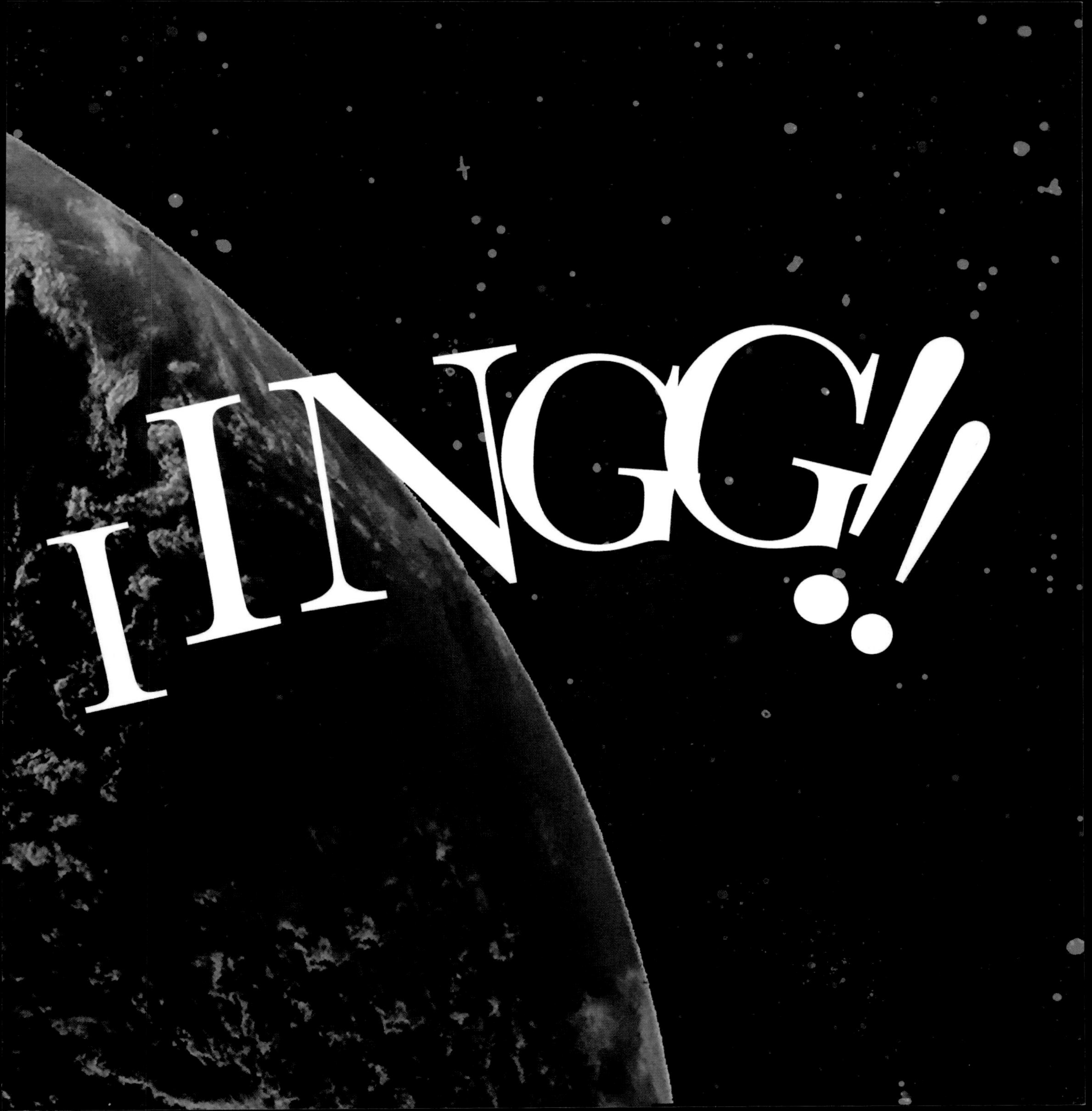
IINGG!!

Luna **soars** through Space,

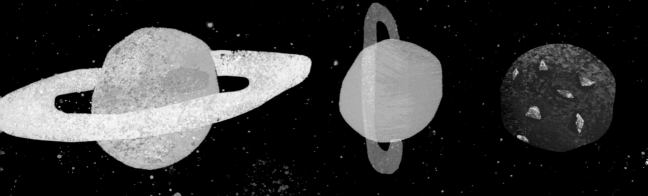

higher and higher!

Crash!!! Luna looks up and sees a mysteriously **amazing** blue world. There are tall royal castles, funny looking buildings,

GIANT ice-creams, mountains made
of diamond and icy lakes.

Suddenly, a creature approaches Luna.

"Hello new being, I am **Zenon**" King of the **Noves**, and you are?"

"Luna", she says.

"What **IS** this place?"

This is Planet Neptune ofcourse miss. Welcome." he says. "Now, I must be going, but please feel free to explore my humble land" and off he went.

So Luna explores as much as she & possibly can.

She thinks
she has explored
**everything**, until
she spots a
**cave**.

She decides
to go
INSIDE.

She goes further into
the cave. It gets

**darker**

and

**darker.**

"Bye Mr Alien Troll Monster!"
and she bounces back home.

Safe and sound,
she lands back in her garden.

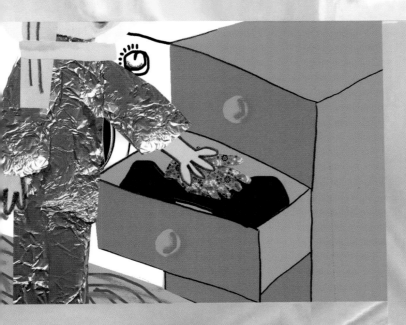

She returns
her **outfit...**

...and

heads

upstairs.

She gets
back into bed
and goes to sleep,
before the night is
over.

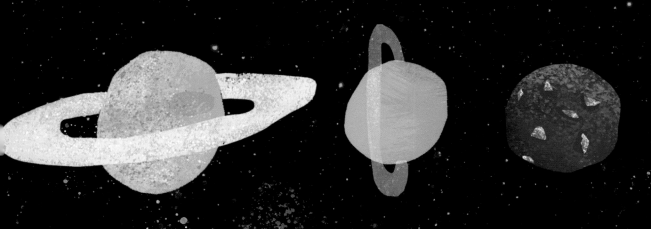